KNOTS

The new compact study guide and identifier

Peter Owen

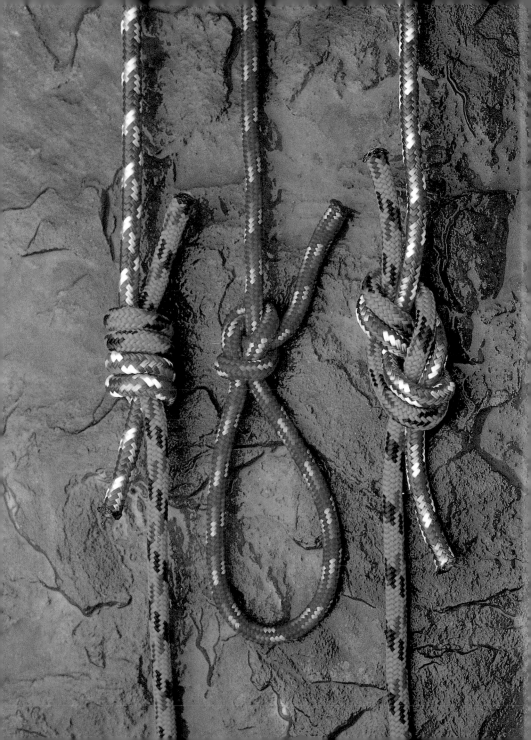

IDENTIFYING

i

KNOTS

The new compact study guide and identifier

Peter Owen

CHARTWELL
BOOKS, INC.

A QUINTET BOOK

Published by Chartwell Books
A Division of Book Sales, Inc.
PO Box 7100
Edison, New Jersey 00837

This edition produced for sale in the U.S.A., its
territories and dependencies only.

ISBN 0-7858-0575-3

This book was designed and produced by
Quintet Publishing Limited
6 Blundell Street
London N7 9BH

Creative Director: Richard Dewing
Designer: Michael Head
Project Editor: Diana Steedman
Illustrator: Peter Owen
Photographers: Paul Forrester, George Steele,
Keith Waterton

Typeset in Great Britain by
Central Southern Typesetters, Eastbourne
Manufactured by Regent Publishing Services Ltd,
Hong Kong
Printed by Leefung-Asco Printers Ltd, China

WARNING
**Synthetic rope melts when heated. Friction may therefore cause the
rope to weaken and break. The result, especially for climbers, could
be fatal. Readers are strongly advised to exercise extreme caution in
situations where synthetic ropes may be exposed to
friction damage.**

CONTENTS

INTRODUCTION

The medium in which knots are tied is normally thought of as thread, string or rope. A general name for all of these is "line".

The knot itself is usually thought of as the intertwining of the ends of that line in such a way as to be secure and suitable for any one of a variety of designated purposes.

Such purposes include the securing of parcels, shoes, boats, climbers and tents among many other uses. Strictly speaking, knots are not just "knots". There are bends and hitches as well. Because these terms are not always used "correctly", there is not a great deal to be gained by knowing the differences. However, it might be of interest to know what they are:

A knot connects both ends of one length of line;

A bend connects two separate lengths of line·

A hitch connects a line to something other than line, such as a wooden spark, tent peg or karabiner.

There are many categories of people who use knots. Indeed, there are few, if any, who do not. Some use knots to ensure that Granny's present arrives intact. Some intend that the tent stays up overnight. Others have a very serious intention of surviving a fall from a rock face. Whichever category is of interest to the reader, it is important to appreciate that any knot will reduce the breaking strain of the line in which it is tied. That is the amount of "pull" under which it will break. At best a knot will reduce the breaking strain to about 85 per cent, at worst to about 15 per cent.

At first sign, the number of knots available can be bewildering. In a classic volume of knots, something like 4,500 are described. Fortunately, most of us can get by if we can tie, and untie, half a dozen or so. A full appreciation of the uses and limitations of a few knots is of far more practical use than a limited understanding of thousands. It is hoped that this book will allow the reader to achieve that modest ambition.

ROPE CONSTRUCTION

A little knowledge of how ropes are made leads to a better understanding of the tying of knots and their limitations in use.

viewed, the strands always go away and twist clockwise. Left-hand laid rope is rarely seen these days, but if it is, the opposite

Traditionally, strands of fibre are twisted together to form a "laid" rope. The number of strands is usually three. The direction in which these strands are twisted determines the lay, which can be right- or left-handed. From whichever end right-hand laid rope is

Whichever way you examine right-hand rope, notice how the strands ascend upwards and to the right. Left-hand laid rope is a rarity.

applies. The strands go away and twist anti-clockwise.

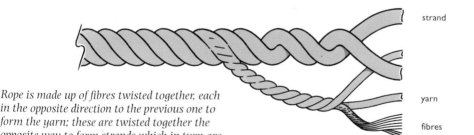

Rope is made up of fibres twisted together, each in the opposite direction to the previous one to form the yarn; these are twisted together the opposite way to form strands which in turn are twisted to form right-laid rope.

strand

yarn

fibres

A closer inspection of stranded rope reveals that its construction is a little more detailed than described above. Right-hand laid rope is made as follows: fibres are twisted together right-handed to make a yarn; yarns are twisted together left-handed to make a strand; strands are twisted together right-

handed to make a rope.

Note especially that at the various stages of construction the twist is reversed. This alternating of the lay ensures that the component parts do not merge into each other. It is this method that provides greater strength to the rope.

NATURAL FIBRE ROPE

Until about the time of World War II, all rope was made from natural materials. These were mainly hemp, manilla, cotton, coir, flax and sisal. Up to that time, ropes were entirely of a laid construction. There have been many different forms of construction other than three-strand right-hand lay. Left-hand laid has been mentioned already. For smoothness, four- and six-strand ropes were made. However, the construction of rope with an even number of strands requires a "heart" to prevent the outer strands collapsing.

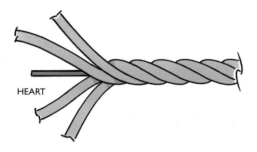

HEART

A significant contribution to the strength of laid ropes can be attributed to the tendency to "unwind" when under strain. The heart of an even-stranded rope, is, of necessity, straight. Consequently, the overall strength of such a rope is limited by the heart's lack of ability to stretch. The result is a relatively poor breaking strain when compared with other constructions.

Each type of construction has served a different purpose, but it is interesting to note that the strongest was found to be three-strand. Today, those other than three-strand, right-hand lay, will rarely be encountered.

Though sharing many problems with modern synthetic rope equivalents, a natural fibre rope does have its own problems. When wet it swells which can make knots very difficult to untie. It also tends to become quite brittle. Elements such as harsh sun and chemicals also cause the rope to deteriorate, as they will a synthetic equivalent.

SYNTHETIC FIBRE ROPES

The strength of a natural fibre rope is limited by the fact that the fibres are relatively short. They do not run the length of the rope. Synthetic fibres can be made much longer, so synthetic fibre ropes are stronger. Other ways in which synthetic fibre ropes differ from their natural fibre equivalents are: size for size they are lighter; they are available in a variety of colours; they have a higher tensile strength; they are capable of absorbing shocks; they are almost immune to rot, mildew and degradation by salt water; they absorb less water and so the breaking strain remains near to constant when wet.

Nylon (polamide) ropes stretch more than any other. This makes them very good at absorbing shock loads. Consequently, they are frequently used for anchoring boats, climbing and towing cars and boats. They do not float.

Polyester ropes are nearly as strong as nylon ropes, but with very little stretch. This makes them eminently suitable for use as halyards and sheets on board sailing boats. Once again, they do not float.

Polypropylene makes a good, relatively

cheap, general purpose rope which does float. It is a relative coarse rope to handle, but sailors use it for such purposes as making and mooring lines.

Polyethylene rope is neither as strong as other types of synthetic rope, nor is it widely used.

Aramide is one of the strongest of the synthetic fibre ropes. It is also one of the most expensive. Ultraviolet rays cause more degradation than on other types, so its use tends to be restricted to those whose primary concern is performance.

A disadvantage of all synthetic fibre ropes is that they are so smooth that some knots are likely to undo themselves. For this reason, it is often advisable to put an extra half hitch or tuck in for added security.

Some synthetic fibre ropes are laid up as stranded ropes in a manner very similar to that used for natural fibre ropes. Others might be braided.

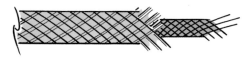

Braided rope usually has a sheath of 16 or more strands surrounding an inner core. This core might be another braided rope, or, perhaps a solid core of parallel, straight fibres. Yet again, sometimes the inner core has a slight twist put in it. Plaited usually describes rope which is formed of solid plaits of four or eight strands.

A potential problem with synthetic fibre ropes is that they melt when overheated. This heat can be generated accidentally simply by the friction of one rope rubbing against an object like a cleat or karabiner, or even against another rope. In an extreme case this could cause the rope to break. It is also possible for enough heat to be generated

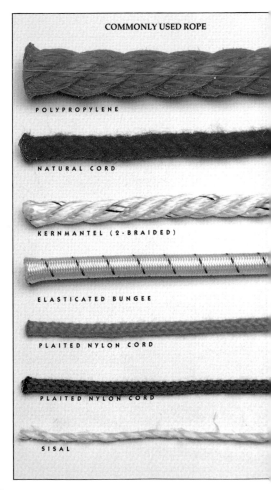

COMMONLY USED ROPE

POLYPROPYLENE

NATURAL CORD

KERNMANTEL (2-BRAIDED)

ELASTICATED BUNGEE

PLAITED NYLON CORD

PLAITED NYLON CORD

SISAL

The breaking strength of a modern rope is well above any force which should be created in a fall. Of more importance to the climber is the rope's ability to absorb the energy of a fall.

by the friction of a knot tightening. The result of this might be, rather than a knot, a fused lump which can never be untied. Ropes, particularly synthetic fibre ropes, should never be allowed to slide through the hands. To do so will encourage painful friction burns. The rope should be let go hand over hand.

All other things being equal, a rope which is twice the diameter of another will be four times as strong. This is because the cross-section area is four times as great. However, it is not necessarily the case that the strongest rope available is the best one to use in any particular set of circumstances. There are often other over-riding requirements. In some circumstances, elasticity may be of more importance than strength. The rope might be required to bear shock loads, for example, in which case one made of polyamide (nylon) would be a good choice. On another occasion a rope which might be just strong enough for a given purpose might be too thin to be handled in comfort.

When buying, steer clear of stiff rope. Time will not make it any more supple. Laid-up rope which is made from relatively thick multifilaments (fibres) which are twisted together will give excellent resistance to wear. At the same time they might be awkward to tie, and knots may not hold well enough to be safe.

For anchoring purposes, sailors should not use a rope that floats, particularly when in harbour. Any rope on the surface will, given time, be severed by the propellers of a passing motor boat. Floating lines should be used only for making fast to quays and pontoons, and for safety lines such as a heaving line or a line attached to a life-ring.

SOME BREAKING STRAINS (KGs)

Material	Diameter			Material	Diameter		
	6mm	8mm	10mm		6mm	8mm	10mm
aramid core	1118	2504	3845	polyester, 16-braid	1000	1704	2604
nylon, 3-strand	750	1354	2086	polypropylene, 3-strand	500	909	1363
polyester, 3-strand	568	1022	1590	polythene, 3-strand	154	700	1091

HOW TO CHOOSE A ROPE

Rope should be chosen according to the situation for which it will be used – considering carefully both the material and the type (braided or laid-up).

Purpose / Material	General purpose	Climbing	Towing	Anchorage	Mooring	Halyards	Fishing
Polyester				X	X	X	
Nylon	X	X	X	X	X		X
Poly-propylene			X		X		

Although not a particularly strong knot, the clove hitch allows the sailor to regulate the length of rope between boat and mooring. It ties best on soft, flexible rope.

11

The obvious use of the Highwayman's hitch is to tether horses, but it is useful in making temporary fastenings in many situations.

SEALING ENDS

When you buy synthetic rope from a chandlery, an electrically heated knife is used to cut the rope to the required length. This gives a sharp edge and seals the end. When you cut synthetic rope yourself, however, you will probably use an ordinary sharp knife and then melt the end of the rope with a cigarette lighter or an electric ring.

LOOKING AFTER ROPE

Rope is expensive so always look after it. Try to avoid dragging it over sharp or rough edges, or over surfaces where particles of dirt and grit will penetrate the fibres. Do not force rope into harsh kinks.

Before coiling it, always make sure that the rope is dry, even if it is synthetic. If it has been in sea water, rinse it with fresh water to remove any deposits of salt. At the end of the season, wash ropes thoroughly in a detergent, carefully removing any oil or tar stains with petrol or trichloroethylene.

Tying knots weakens ropes. The sharper the curve and the tighter the nip, the greater is the chance that the rope will break, and when it does so it will break immediately outside the knot. Many often-used knots are surprisingly harmful to rope, the worst offender being the simple overhand knot (see page 16). Never use two ropes of different materials together because only the more rigid of the two will work under strain.

COILING A ROPE

The function of coiling is that the rope will be immediately accessible and untangled when needed. Coiled rope is useful if you want to sling the rope on your rucksack or over your shoulder.

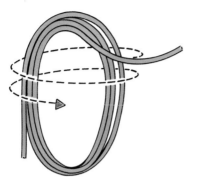

SELECTING KNOTS

One of the main reasons for selecting one knot rather than another is the relative strength of the knots. This is especially true for climbers and mountaineers, but it is also a consideration for mariners. Other characteristics such as speed and ease of tying, bulk and reliability will also influence the choice.

Climbers generally use knots that are bulky and that have several wrapping turns, which are designed to absorb strains and to avoid weakening the rope unnecessarily. Knots used by climbers must be checked regularly, especially if stiff rope is used, because it is more difficult to tie than more flexible line and the knots may be less secure.

Anglers use similar, but much smaller, barrel-shaped knots, partly to improve their chances of a good catch and partly to safeguard expensive fishing tackle.

Generally, you should also untie knots as soon as possible after use. This will be easier if you choose a suitable knot in the first place. And remember that knots that disappear when they are slipped off their foundations such as the clove hitch and Prussic knot (see pages 27 and 35) are no less strong or secure.

Finally, remember that tying knots requires practice. You must be able to tie them quickly and easily when you are halfway up a mountain or at sea. The only way to gain the necessary skill and confidence is to practise each knot over and over again until the steps become automatic and you do not have to think about them. In some circumstances your life or the lives of your companions could depend on it.

ROPE PARTS

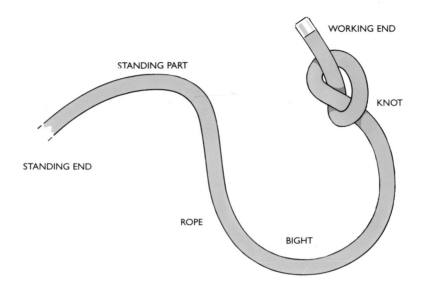

WORKING END

STANDING PART

KNOT

STANDING END

ROPE

BIGHT

HOW TO USE THIS BOOK

The diagrams that accompany the descriptions of the knots are intended to be self-explanatory. The arrows indicate the directions in which you should push or pull the working ends of your line, while the dotted lines indicate intermediate positions of the rope. Always follow the order indicated of going over or under a length of line; reversing this order could result in a completely different knot. The knots in this book can be used in different situations: general purpose, climbing, camping, sailing and fishing; these are shown below as symbols. Each knot in the book is accompanied by the relevant symbol/s; designed to give you at-a-glance information about the uses of a particular knot.

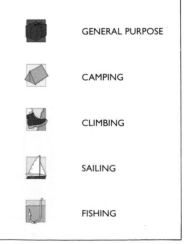

GENERAL PURPOSE

CAMPING

CLIMBING

SAILING

FISHING

STOPPER KNOTS

OVERHAND KNOT

OVERHAND LOOP

MULTIPLE
OVERHAND KNOT

HEAVING LINE
KNOT

FIGURE-OF-EIGHT
KNOT

This group of knots is most often used to prevent the end of a length of rope, string or small stuff slipping through an eye or a hole. Stopper knots can also be used to bind the end of a line so that it will not unravel, and they can also be used as decoration. At sea they are frequently used to weight lines or on running rigging, and they are also used by climbers, campers and fishermen.
The simple overhand knot, which is the basis of so many other knots, is a stopper knot. Sailors tend to use the figure-of-eight knot for general use and multiple overhand knots to weigh down or decorate the ends of knots.

OVERHAND KNOT

Also known as: THUMB KNOT

This is the knot that forms the basis of most other knots. In its own right it is used as a simple stopper knot in the end of a line. It is not, however, widely used by sailors as it is extremely difficult to untie when the rope is wet. Tight overhand knots on small stuff can also be difficult to undo.

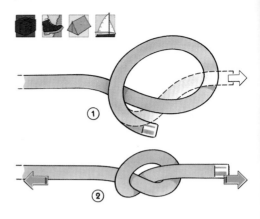

OVERHAND LOOP

This is a rather ungainly knot, but it is extremely useful in circumstances where a bulky stopper is required. It is, in fact, the loop that most people would tie without thinking if they needed to fasten a knot in the end of a length of string. The drawback is that the line will probably have to be cut because the knot is difficult to untie.

16

MULTIPLE OVERHAND KNOT

Also known as: BLOOD KNOT

This knot's alternative name has a rather gruesome derivation: the knot used to be tied in the ends of the lashes of the cat o'nine tails, the whip used for flogging in both the British Army and Navy until the punishment's official abolition in 1948. A far less grisly use is as a weight in the cords with which Capuchin monks tie their habits.

Sailors use the knot as a stopper or weighting knot on small stuff, although it is difficult to untie when the line is wet.

When you tie the knot, keep the loop open and slack, and then pull gently on both ends of the line simultaneously, twisting the two ends in opposite directions as you do so.

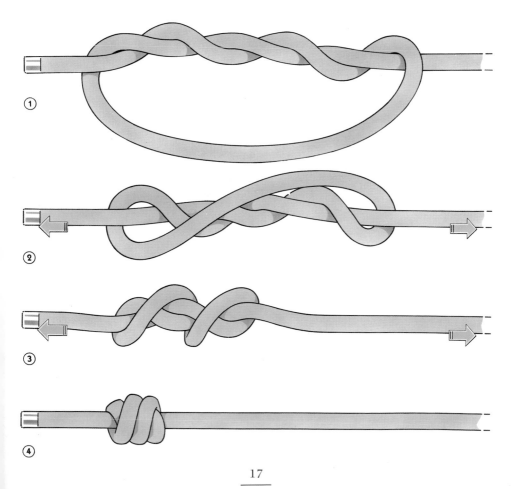

HEAVING LINE KNOT

Also known as: FRANCISCAN KNOT, MONK'S KNOT

Sailors find this knot useful when a heavy line is to be thrown ashore or aboard another boat. It is attached to a heaving line – that is, a light line – which can be thrown ahead so that the heavier line can be pulled across the gap. The knot is tied to the end of the lighter line to give it the necessary additional weight. Heaving lines are usually 10–15mm (½–⅜in) in diameter and may be up to 25m (80ft) long. They should float and be flexible, and it is important that they be strong enough to bear a man's weight. The knot's alternative names derive from its use to weight the ends of the cords that Franciscan monks use as belts.

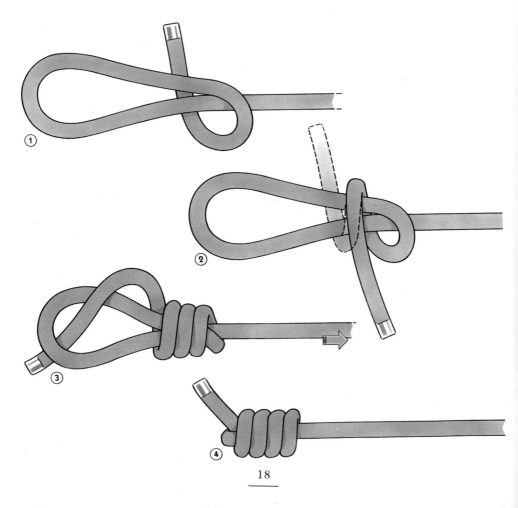

18

FIGURE-OF-EIGHT KNOT

Also known as: FLEMISH KNOT, SAVOY KNOT

This interlacing knot has for long been regarded as an emblem of interwoven affection, appearing in heraldry as the symbol of faithful love. It also appears in the arms of the House of Savoy.

The knot, which is made in the end of a line, with the upper loop around the standing part and the lower loop around the working end, is widely used by sailors on the running rigging.

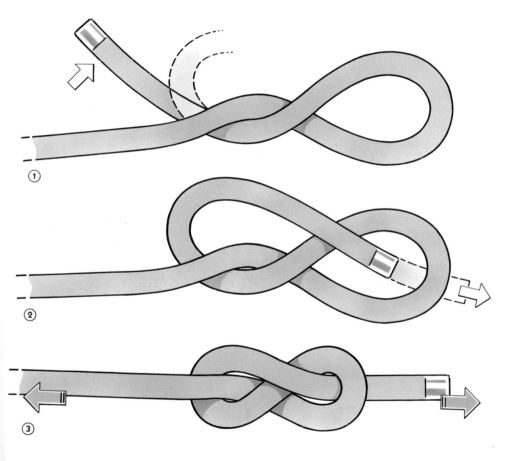

FIGURE-OF-EIGHT CHAIN

This popular decorative chain can be made, quite simply, by making a series of figure-of-eight knots all in the same direction. It can be used as a belt or strap for a shoulder bag.

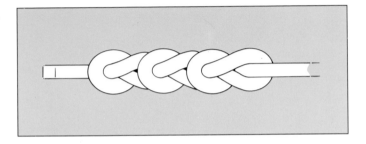

HITCHES

HIGHWAYMAN'S HITCH

TIMBER HITCH

CONSTRICTOR KNOT

CLOVE HITCH

Hitches are knots that are used to secure a rope to a post, hook, ring, spar or rail or to another rope that plays no part in the actual tying. Hitches do not keep their shape on their own. Because they are often used by sailors for mooring, lashing and fastening, they must be able to withstand parallel strain.

FISHERMAN'S BEND

ROUND TURN AND TWO HALF HITCHES

ITALIAN HITCH

PRUSSIC KNOT

HIGHWAYMAN'S HITCH

Also known as: DRAW HITCH

The name highwayman's hitch comes from the fact the knot was supposedly used by robbers to ensure a swift release for their horses' reins and thus a rapid get-away. A single pull on the working end unties the knot, but the stand part can safely be put under tension.

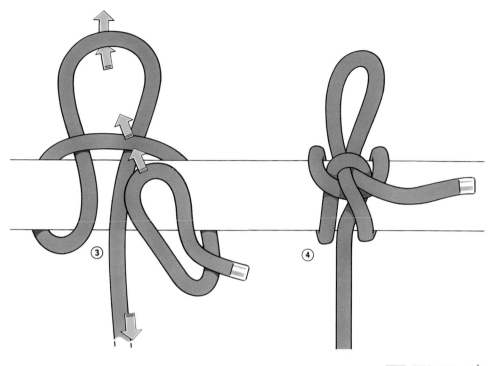

HALF HITCH

The half hitch is among the most widely used of fastenings, but it is, in fact, a temporary knot, formed of a single hitch made around the standing part of another hitch – as in a round turn and two half hitches, for example. The knot is not meant to take any strain but is rather used to complete and strengthen other knots, which may then be used for tying, hanging or hooking.

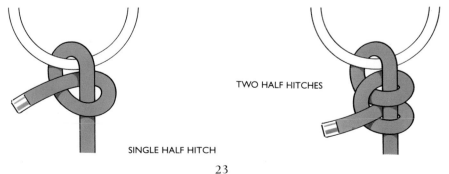

SINGLE HALF HITCH

TWO HALF HITCHES

TRANSOM KNOT

Gardeners will find the transom knot
particularly useful for making trellises or
tying up bean poles. It is similar to the
constrictor knot (see page 25), and, as with
that knot, the ends may be trimmed off for
neatness. Although it can be prised undone,
it is probably easier simply to cut through
the diagonal, when the two halves will fall
apart.

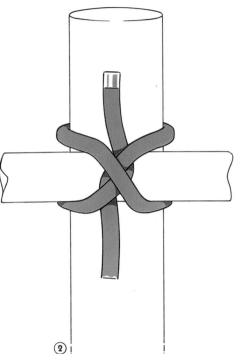

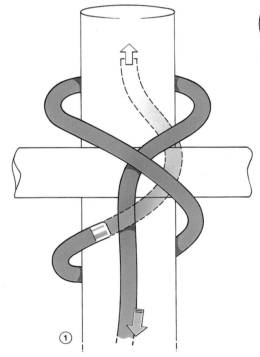

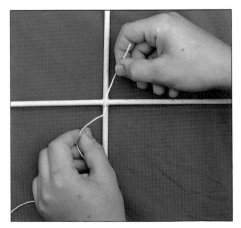

*Tying together the cross-bars
of a kite is best done with a
Transom knot.*

CONSTRICTOR KNOT

This knot has grown in popularity in recent years, and it has dozens of uses. It can be used on the ends of ropes as permanent or temporary whipping; it can be used to secure fabric bags such as those containing *bouquet garni*; it can be used in woodworking to hold two pieces in position while the glue dries.

The knot is formed from an overhand knot, trapped beneath a crosswise round turn, which holds it firmly in place. The constrictor knot will stay tied and grip firmly, and, in fact, the rope may have to be cut free unless the last tuck is made with a bight to produce a slipped knot.

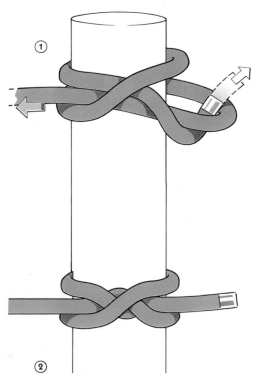

COW HITCH

Also known as: LANYARD HITCH

This hitch, composed of two single hitches, is generally made around a ring and is probably the least secure of all the hitches, and it should be regarded as only a temporary fastening. Its name suggests its most common use – as a means of tethering livestock.

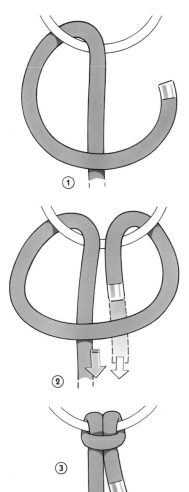

TIMBER HITCH

This distinctive-looking knot is really only a temporary noose, formed by twisting the working end around it sown part and *not* around the standing part. Three twists are usually sufficient to secure the rope around such objects as tree trunks, planks or poles so that they may be raised or lowered or dragged or pulled. More twists may be needed if the object to be moved is especially thick. Unfortunately, this knot is easily tied incorrectly.

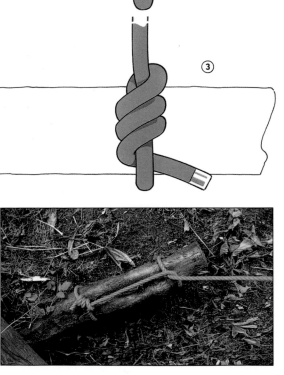

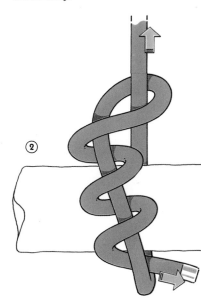

When a single hitch is added to the nearer end of a log or spar, with a timber hitch at the further end, the resulting Killick hitch enables the load to be dragged without it swinging around.

CLOVE HITCH

Also known as: BOATMAN'S KNOT, PEG KNOT

The name clove hitch first appeared in Falconer's *Dictionary of the Marine* in the 18th century, but the knot was probably known for centuries before then.

The main advantage of the clove hitch is that, given practice, it can be tied around a post with just one hand, which makes it particularly useful for sailors who may, for example, need to tie a dinghy to a bollard with one hand while holding onto a guard rail with the other. Although it is often recommended as a mooring knot, the clove

hitch is not, however, totally secure if the strain is intermittent and at an inconstant angle, and while it will afford a temporary hold, it should be replaced by something more stable as soon as is practicable. Adding a stopper knot or making one or two half hitches around the standing part of the rope will make the knot more secure.

Campers often use it to secure tent poles, which is the origin of one of its alternative names, the peg knot.

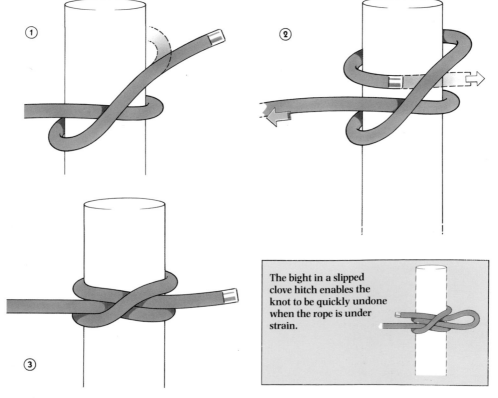

The bight in a slipped clove hitch enables the knot to be quickly undone when the rope is under strain.

CLOVE HITCH, DROPPED OVER A POST

The knot formed when two overlapping half hitches are dropped over a post is widely used in sailing for mooring to bollards on quaysides. It is also useful in camping for tightening guy ropes.

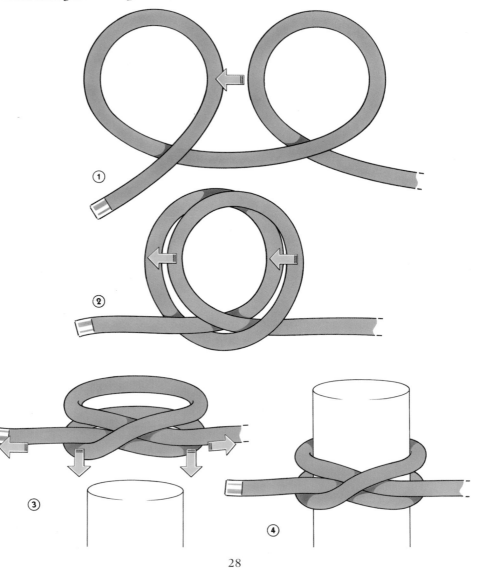

CLOVE HITCH, MADE ON A RING

This particular version of the clove hitch is more commonly used in mountaineering than in sailing, for in sailing the ring is usually narrower than the rope, which can become badly chafed and therefore dangerous. Climbers use it to regulate the length of rope between the climber and the piton (that is, the peg or spike driven into rock or a crack to support the rope).

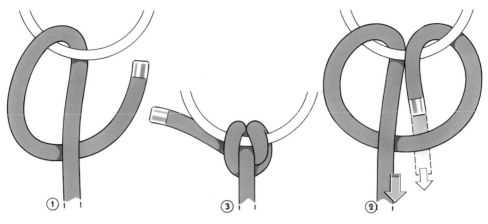

FISHERMEN'S BEND

Also known as: ANCHOR BEND

If the cow hitch is the least secure of the hitches, the fisherman's bend is the most stable. Simply formed by making two turns around the post or through the ring and then tucking the working end through both turns, the knot is widely used by sailors to moor their boats at the quayside. Extra security can be provided by adding a half hitch.

The knot's other name – the anchor bend – derives from the fact that sailors use it to tie on the anchor ring, although a stopper knot should be added for safety's sake.

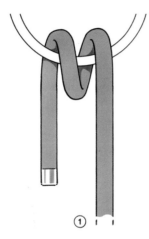

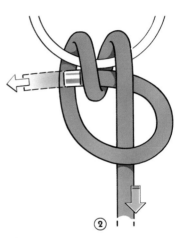

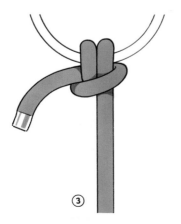

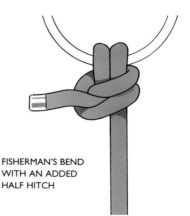

FISHERMAN'S BEND
WITH AN ADDED
HALF HITCH

HITCHES

CAT'S PAW

Because the strain is equal on both sides, this is the best hook knot for rope of medium diameter. It has long been used by dock workers and sailors to sling heavy loads, and the name cat's paw has been current since at least the early 18th century. When a single part of a loaded rope is hung over a hook, the line is weakened by about one-third. A cat's paw, securely drawn up, gives the additional assurance that, should one leg break, the other will last long enough to allow the load to be safely lowered to the ground.

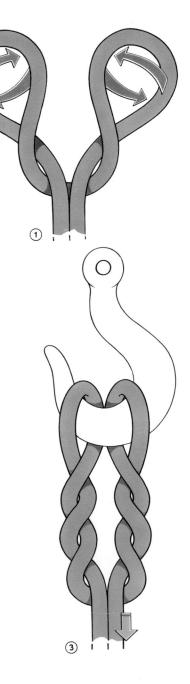

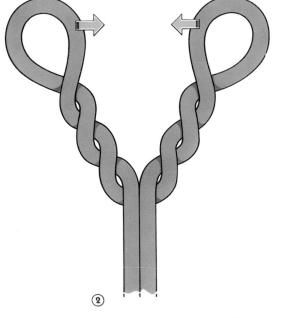

31

BILL HITCH

This knot can be made and untied easily, and it is suitable for use with large diameter ropes. It is not, however, used for sailing purposes very much and tends to be associated with camping activities. It is good for hoisting light objects aloft.

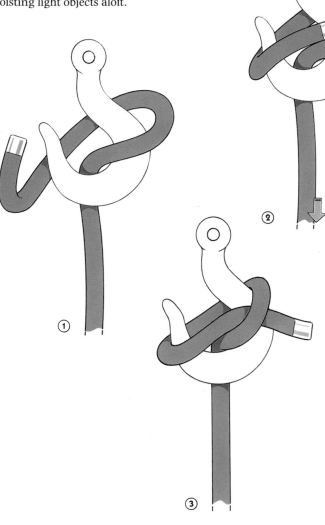

ROLLING HITCH

Also known as: MAGNER'S HITCH, MAGNUS HITCH

This useful knot is basically a clove hitch with the first turn repeated. It is employed by both mariners and mountaineers and is the most effective way of securing a small rope to a larger line that is under strain. As long as the smaller rope is perpendicular to the larger, the knot will slide easily along; once tension is exerted on the standing part and working end of the smaller rope, the knot locks in position. If you place your hand over the knot and slide it along the thicker line it will slide off the end and uncoil into a straight length of rope.

The name rolling hitch has been used since the 1840s; before then the knot was known as magner's or magnus hitch.

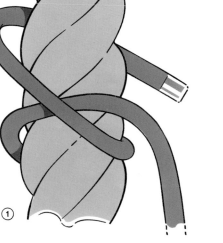

(1)

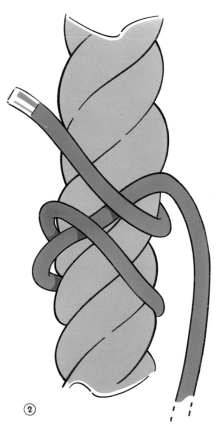

(2)

ROUND TURN AND TWO HALF HITCHES

Use this versatile knot whenever you need to fasten a line to a ring, hook, handle, pole, rail or beam. It is a strong, dependable knot, which never jams. It has the additional advantage that once one end has been secured with a round turn and two half hitches, the other end can be tied with a second knot, which makes it invaluable for fastening unwieldy objects to car roof racks.

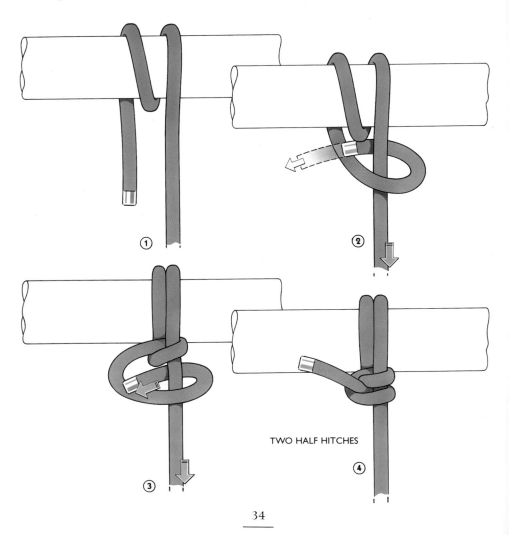

TWO HALF HITCHES

34

PRUSSIC KNOT

The knot is named after Dr. Carl Prussik, who devised it in 1931. It is used by climbers to attach slings to a rope. With downward pressure the knot jams. When the weight is taken off it it frees itself and can be pushed up the rope. Used in pairs, it is possible to work one's way up a rope by alternating the weight between one sling and the other.

The knot must be tied with a sling which is significantly smaller than the rope around which it is tied.

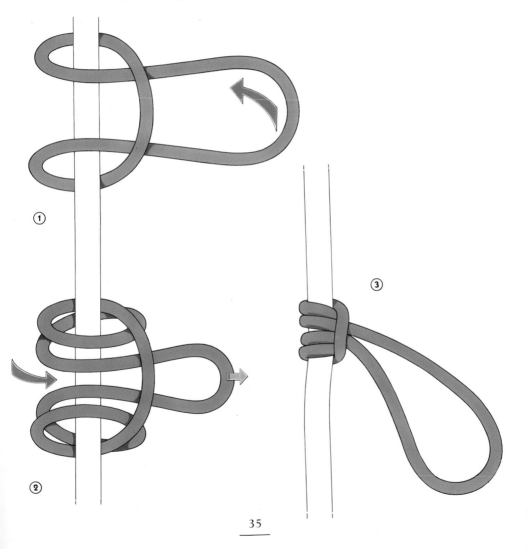

ITALIAN HITCH

Also known as: MUNTER FRICTION HITCH, SLIDING RING HITCH

This addition to the mountaineers' lexicon of knots was introduced in 1974, and it is the official means of belaying (that is, fixing a running rope around a rock or a cleat) of the Union Internationale des Associations d'Alpinisme. The rope is passed around and through a karabiner and will check a climber's fall by locking up. Alternatively, the rope can be paid out or pulled in to provide slack or tension as required.

The major disadvantage of the knot is that it is easy to tie incorrectly.

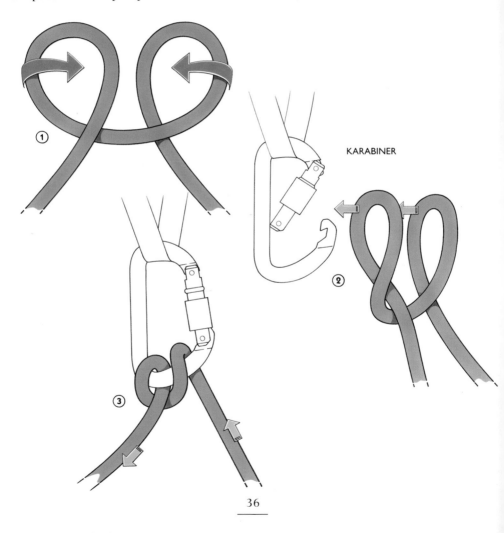

KARABINER

Loops

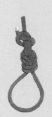

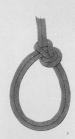

Loops are made to be dropped over an object, unlike hitches, which are made directly around the object and follow its shape. They are knots formed by folding back the end of a rope or line into an eye or loop and then fastening it to its standing part so that the knot is fixed and does not move.

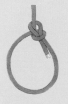

THREADED FIGURE-OF-EIGHT

BOWLINE

CLIMBER'S BOWLINE

BOWLINE, ON A BIGHT

SPANISH BOWLINE

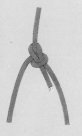

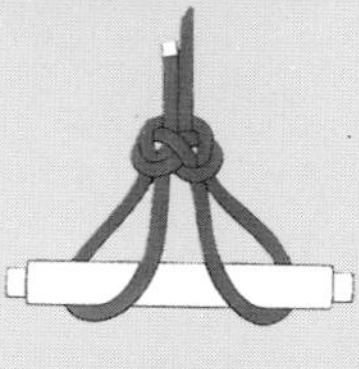

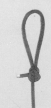

ANGLER'S LOOP

FIGURE-OF-EIGHT LOOP

Also known as: FIGURE-OF-EIGHT ON THE BIGHT

Although this knot is difficult to adjust and cannot easily be untied after loading, its advantages outweigh these drawbacks. It is a comparatively simple knot to tie, and it stays tied, even when stiff rope is used. In addition, because its appearance is unmistakable, it can be quickly checked, which is important when it is used by climbers.

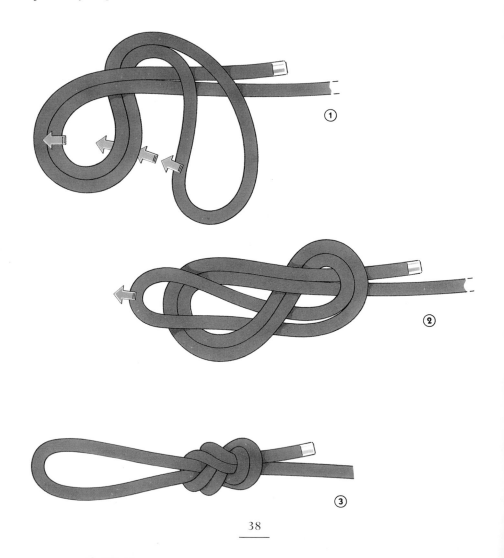

①

②

③

THREADED FIGURE-OF-EIGHT

This is a variation of the figure-of-eight loop. The most frequent uses of the threaded figure-of-eight are for tying on to the rope and for anchoring non-climbing members of a team.

This is probably the commonest way of attaching rope to the harness. Tying-on using a Bowline is equally satisfactory, but not as popular.

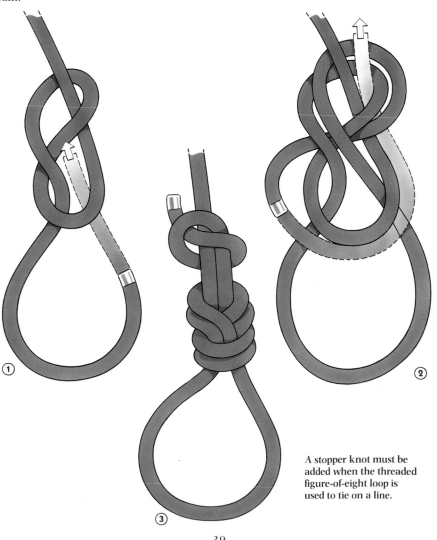

① ② ③

A stopper knot must be added when the threaded figure-of-eight loop is used to tie on to a line.

BOWLINE

The bowline is simple, strong and stable. It is one of the best known and most widely used of knots, especially among sailors, and is generally tied to form a fixed loop at the end of a line or to attach a rope to an object. At sea it is used on running rigging and for hoisting, joining and salvage work.

Tie a bowline by forming a loop in the standing part of the line. Pass the working end up through the eye of the loop, around the back of the standing part and then down through the eye again. For safety's sake, finish the bowline off with a stopper knot to prevent it from turning into a slip knot.

Among the knot's advantages are the facts that it does not slip, come loose or jam and that it can be quickly and easily untied, even when the line is under tension. A major disadvantage can be that if it is tied with stiff rope, it is liable to work loose as the line cannot "bed down" properly.

The running bowline makes a noose that falls open as soon as the tension is removed from the line. The left-handed bowline is not as secure as the bowline itself and should be avoided.

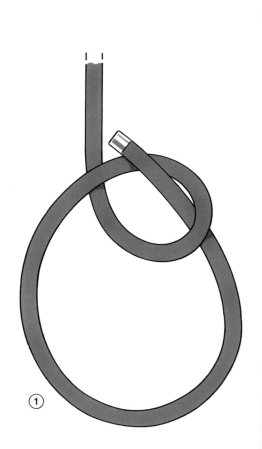

(1)

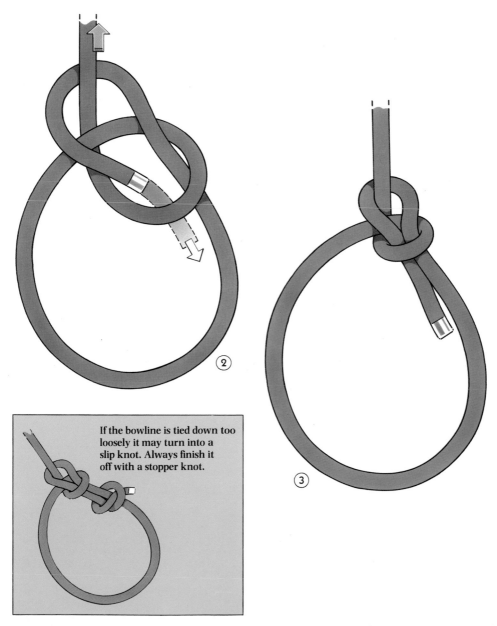

If the bowline is tied down too loosely it may turn into a slip knot. Always finish it off with a stopper knot.

BOWLINE, CASTING METHOD

Use the method of tying a bowline illustrated here when you need to fasten a line around an object. When synthetic rope is used to tie this knot, it might be less reliable. It is a good idea to secure the end with an extra half-hitch, or tuck it and trap it beneath one of the rope's strands.

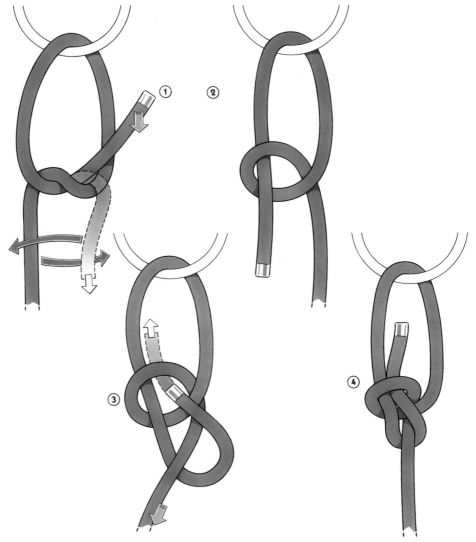

CLIMBER'S BOWLINE

Also known as: BULIN KNOT

Climbers use the bowline – which is known by them as the bulin knot – as a safety measure during ascents, when it is clipped into the karabiner.

Climbers also tie this knot directly around their waists so that they can adjust the length of line before undertaking an ascent. When ever it is used in this way, the knot must be finished off with a stopper knot.

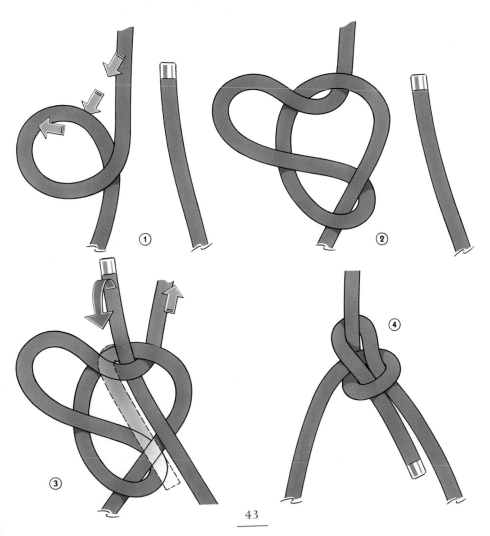

BOWLINE ON A BIGHT

This is an ancient knot, but one that is still in use today, especially in sea rescues. If the person who is being rescued is conscious, he or she places a leg through each loop and hangs on to the standing part.

If the casualty is unconscious, both legs are placed through one loop while the other loop is passed under the armpits. The knot is equally suitable for salvaging inanimate objects.

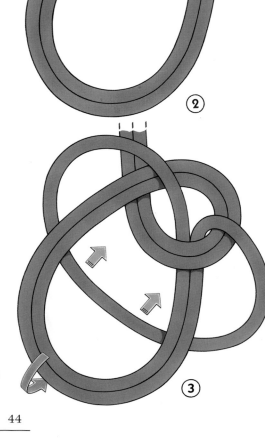

① ② ③

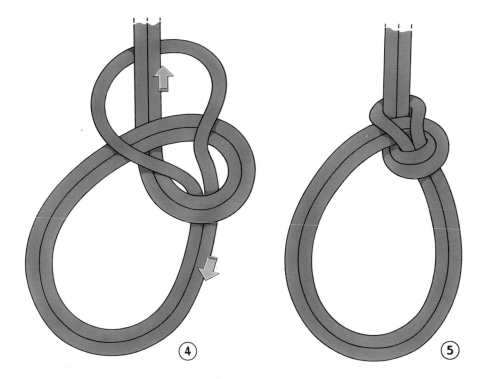

④ ⑤

SPANISH BOWLINE

Also known as: CHAIR KNOT

This is an extremely strong knot that is used by fire brigades (when it is known as the chair knot), coastguards and mountain rescuers. Like the bowline on a bight, it is an ancient knot, which is formed of two separate and independent loops that hold securely, even under considerable strain. One loop is slipped over the casualty's head, around the back and under the armpits; the other loop goes around both legs, just behind the knees. It is vital that each loop is adjusted to size and locked into position, otherwise an unconscious casualty could easily fall – perhaps to his or her death – through the loops.

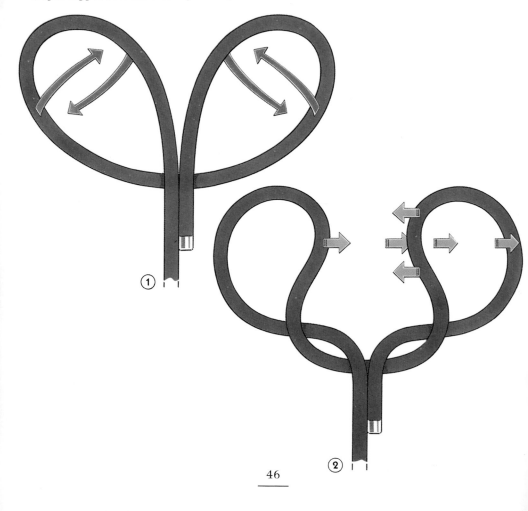

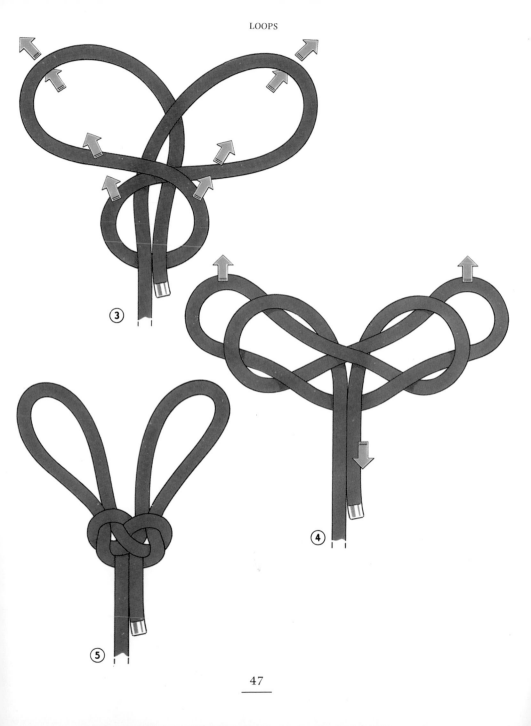

③

④

⑤

ANGLER'S LOOP

Also known as: PERFECTION LOOP

The angler's loop is known to have been in use since the 1870s. It is, as its name suggests, most frequently employed by fishermen. In addition to fishing line, it can be tied with string or fine synthetic line. Authorities differ about whether it is a suitable knot for rope. It is difficult to untie, which may militate against its use at sea, and it is prone to jam. It is also a rather bulky knot.

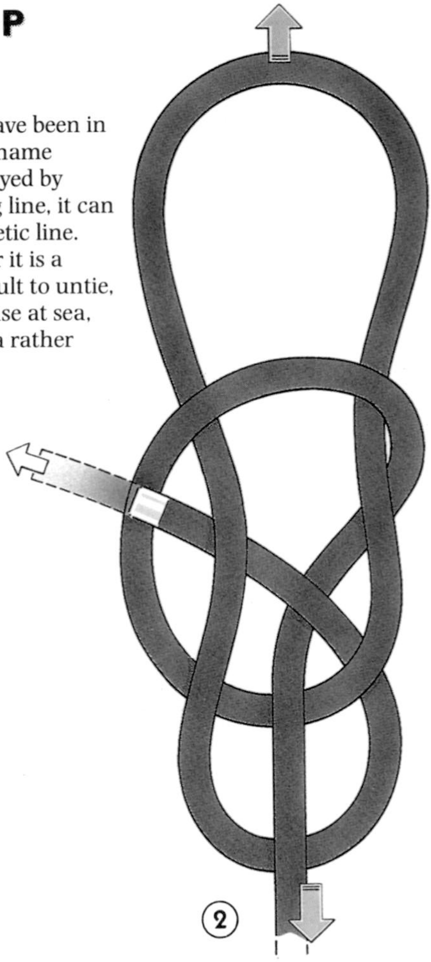

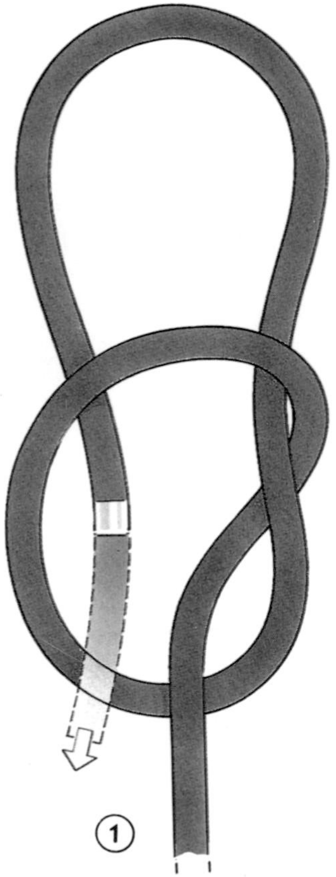

①

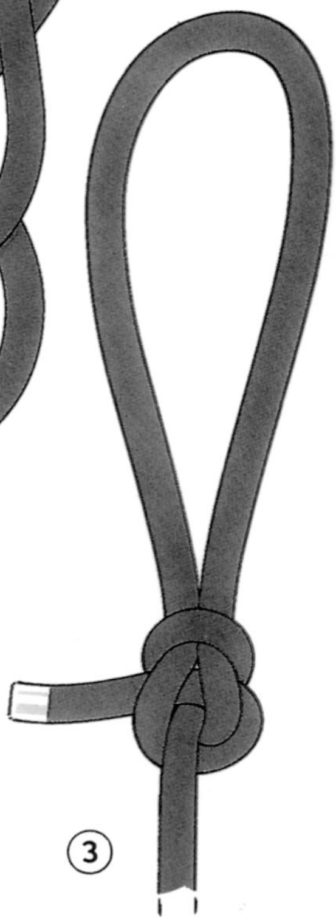

②

③

48

BENDS

Bends are used to join the ends of two lengths of rope to form one longer piece. Ideally, to ensure that the knot is secure, the two ropes that are to be joined should be of the same kind and have the same diameter. Unusually however, the sheet bend (see page 56) is secure even when it is used to join ropes of different diameters.

REEF KNOT

CAPSIZED REEF KNOT

THIEF KNOT

SURGEON'S KNOT

FISHERMAN'S KNOT

DOUBLE FISHERMAN'S KNOT

HUNTER'S BEND

SHEET BEND

FIGURE-OF-EIGHT BEND

CARRICK BEND

REEF KNOT

Also known as: SQUARE KNOT

This is an ancient knot, which was known during the Late Stone Age. The Ancient Greeks knew it as the Hercules knot, and it was also tied in Ancient Rome. It is often the only knot – apart from the granny knot – that many people know, and when the ends are only partly drawn through the knot to leave loops and to form a double reef bow, it is frequently used to tie shoe laces. Its traditional and proper use is to join the two ends of a rope when reefing a sail.

Both short ends of the knot are on the same side – if they are not, it is a thief knot – and the knot is flat – if it is not, it is a granny knot. The reef knot is more secure than both the thief knot and the granny knot, but it should be used only as a temporary measure and with lines of the same diameter that will not be subject to strain. If it has to be used with lines that will bear considerable weight, stopper knots should be tied in the short ends.

②

③

①

④

The Reef knot is a multi-purpose knot which is symmetrical and made from two interlocked bights. Its beauty lies in its simplicity.

CAPSIZED REEF KNOT

Also known as: LARK'S HEAD KNOT, CAPSIZED SQUARE KNOT

The reef of a sail is that part which is rolled and tied up by the reef points to reduce the area caught by the wind, and the ease with which a reef knot can be slipped apart make it perfect for reefing sails. When one end of a reef knot is pulled sharply or is subjected to strain, the knot will untie and become unstable. Capsized reef knots have caused accidents and should be used with caution.

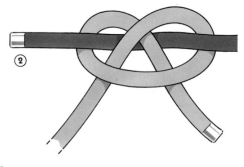

51

THIEF KNOT

According to legend sailors on whaling ships used this knot to tie their clothes bags. Thieves would retie them with reef knots, thus revealing that the bags had been burgled. The thief knot is very similar to the reef knot, but the short ends are on opposite sides.

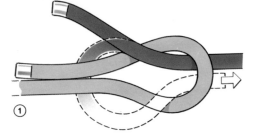

SURGEON'S KNOT

As its name suggests, this knot is used by surgeons to tie off blood vessels, and it seems to have been in use since about the end of World War II. The knot has a good grip, twisting as it is drawn up and the diagonal is wrapped around it. It is less bulky and flatter than some of the other knots used by surgeons – the carrick bend and the reef knot, for instance – which tend to leave visible scars.

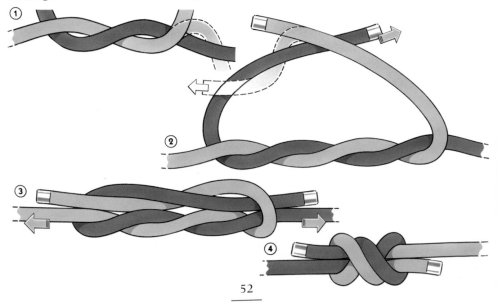

FISHERMAN'S KNOT

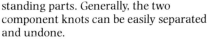

Also known as: ANGLER'S KNOT, ENGLISH KNOT,
ENGLISHMAN'S BEND OR KNOT, HALIBUT KNOT,
TRUE-LOVER'S BEND OR KNOT, WATERMAN'S KNOT

The fisherman's knot should not be confused with the fisherman's bend (which is actually a hitch, see page 30). They are quite different knots. This knot was invented during the 19th century, although some writers have suggested that it may have been known to the Ancient Greeks. It is formed from two identical overhand knots, which are pushed against each other so that the short, working ends of the ropes lie in opposite directions, almost parallel to their standing parts. Generally, the two component knots can be easily separated and undone.

It should be used to join lines of equal diameter, but it is not suitable for ropes with large or even medium diameters. It is widely used by anglers to join fishing line, and it is also suitable for string and twine. The knot is not, in fact, as strong as the line from which it is formed when it is under great strain.

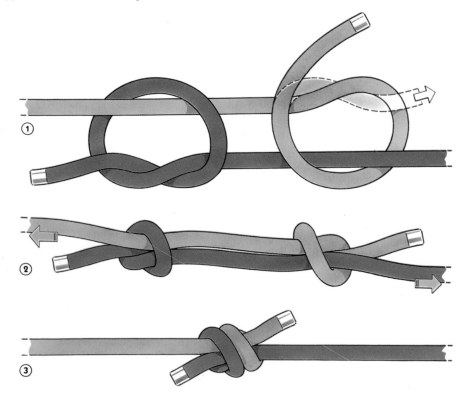

DOUBLE FISHERMAN'S KNOT

Also known as: GRAPEVINE KNOT

This is one of the strongest knots for joining ropes or for forming slings, and it is used not only, as its name suggests, by anglers to secure their lines but also by climbers on small stuff. It is a comparatively bulky knot and is not, for that reason, suitable for anything more substantial than thin line or string. The ends can be taped or seized to the working parts to minimize the risk of the knot working loose.

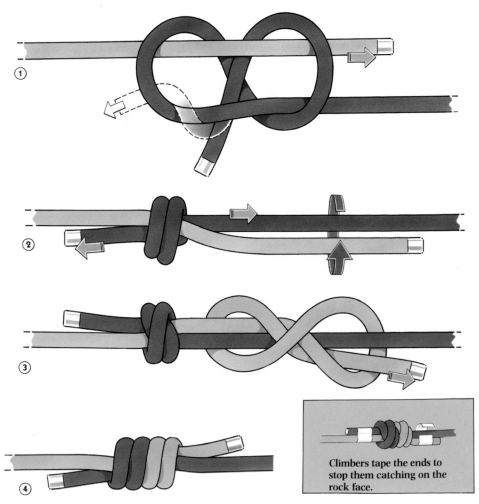

Climbers tape the ends to stop them catching on the rock face.

HUNTER'S BEND

Also known as: RIGGER'S BEND

On 6 October 1968 *The Times* carried a report on the front page describing how Dr Edward Hunter, a retired physician, had invented a new knot. The article generated a lot of interest in both Europe and the United States, but at the height of the publicity it was found that the knot had already been described by Phil D. Smith, an American, in about 1950 in a publication called *Knots for Mountaineers*. Phil Smith had been working on the waterfront in San Francisco during World War II when he had devised the knot, which he had named a rigger's bend.

It is also easy to untie. It is based on two overhand knots and is stronger than the fisherman's bend, the sheet bend and the reef knot, although it is not as strong as the blood knot.

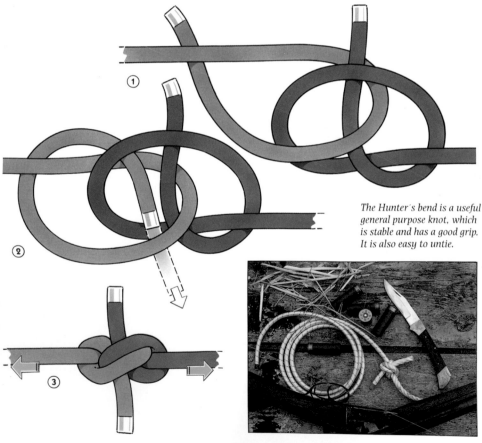

The Hunter's bend is a useful general purpose knot, which is stable and has a good grip. It is also easy to untie.

SHEET BEND

Also known as: COMMON BEND, FLAG BEND

The sheet bend is unusual in that it can be used to join lines of unequal diameters. It is probably the most often used of all the bends, but it is not 100 per cent secure and should never be used in circumstances where it is going to be subject to great strain. Its breaking strain is further reduced in proportion to the difference in the diameters of the lines joined.

Although the knot may be seen in Ancient Egyptian paintings, the name did not appear in print until 1794. The sheet was originally the rope attached to the clew (the lower or after corner) of a sail, which was used for trimming the sail, and it was from this usage that the knot derived its name. It is also traditionally used to join the two corners of a flag to the rope used for raising or lowering it. On such occasions it is sometimes referred to as a flag bend. It can also be used to make a rope fast to anything with an aperture – a handle on a spade, for example – through which the line can be passed and trapped under itself. When the knot is tied with the short ends on opposite sides it becomes a left-handed sheet bend, but this is to be avoided as this knot is not secure.

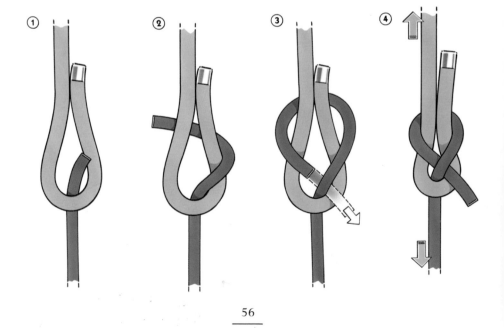

FIGURE-OF-EIGHT BEND

Also known as: FLEMISH BEND OR KNOT

Although this is a simple knot to tie – simply make a figure-of-eight knot in one end and follow it around with the other working end – it is one of the strongest bends that can be tied in both rope and string.

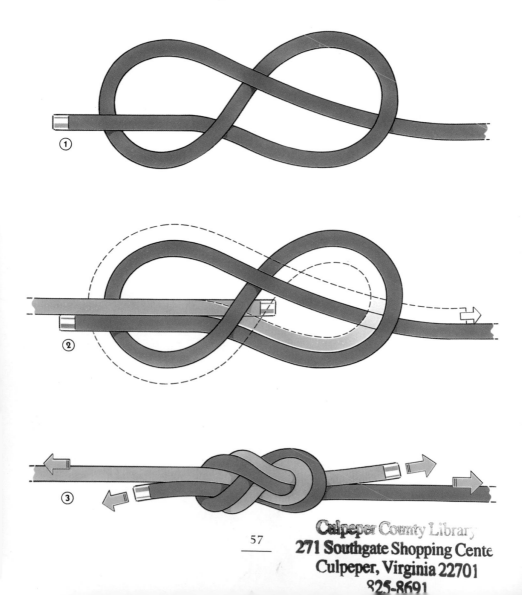

CARRICK BEND

Also known as: COWBOY KNOT, SPLIT KNOT, WARP KNOT

This stable knot, which is formed from two overhand loops crossing each other, was the most widely used knot on old sailing ships. Its common names suggest some of the other circumstances in which the carrick bend may be found – it is known as the cowboy knot to cowhands, the split knot to knitwear manufacturers and the warp knot to sailors.

Today, however, it is less often used aboard ship because it can be difficult to untie when the rope is wet. When it is used, its main purpose is to join large-diameter hawsers and warps, and in these circumstances it is usually left in its flat form with the ends seized (that is, secured by binding with turns of yarn) to the standing parts. In its flat form it is sometimes also used to fasten scarves and belts, and its symmetrical appearance has made it a great favourite with illustrators of military uniforms.

When it is drawn up it capsizes into a completely different shape, and for this reason, although it has been recommended as a knot for mountaineers, it may be unsuitable as it is probably too bulky to pass through a karabiner.

RUNNING KNOTS

RUNNING BOWLINE

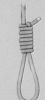

HANGMAN'S KNOT

NOOSE

Running knots are also known as slip knots or nooses. Their main characteristics are that they tighten around the objects on which they are tied but slacken when the strain is reduced. This group of knots is divided into two kinds: those that are tied by passing a bight through a fixed loop at the end of a line and those that are formed from a closed bight knotted at the end of a line or along it. Running knots must be among the oldest knots known to man. They were used in prehistoric times to make weapons and snares to trap animals.

RUNNING BOWLINE

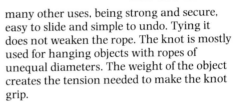

This is probably the only running knot to be used by mariners. It is found on the running rigging or it may be used to raise floating objects that have fallen overboard.

At sea during the 19th century it was used to tighten the squaresail to the yardarm in high winds, and at the same time in the country it was used by poachers. It has many other uses, being strong and secure, easy to slide and simple to undo. Tying it does not weaken the rope. The knot is mostly used for hanging objects with ropes of unequal diameters. The weight of the object creates the tension needed to make the knot grip.

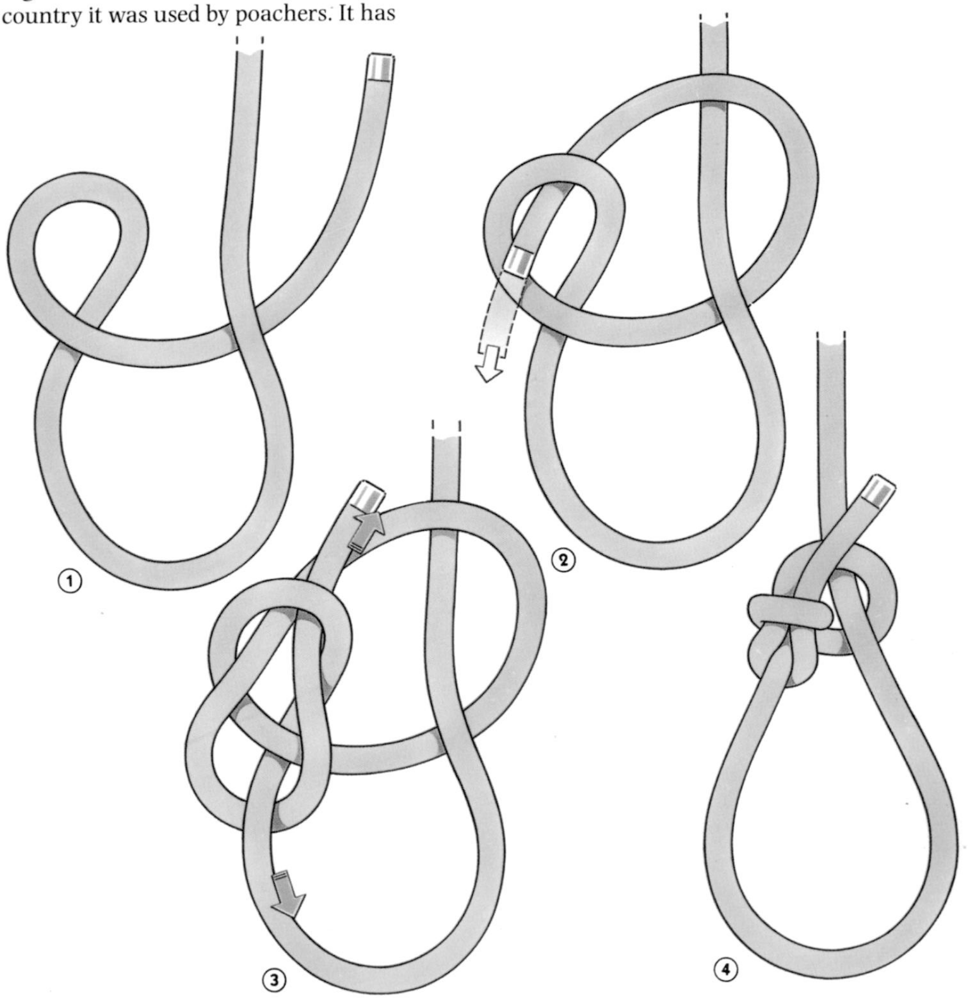

①

②

③

④

HANGMAN'S KNOT

Also known as: JACK KETCH'S KNOT

This knot is one of the running knots that is formed by knotting a closed bight at the end of a line. Its name reveals its macabre use, and its alternative name comes from the notorious hangman and executioner Jack

Ketch, who died in 1686. It is a strong noose, which slides easily. The number of turns can vary between seven and thirteen, although an odd number should always be used.

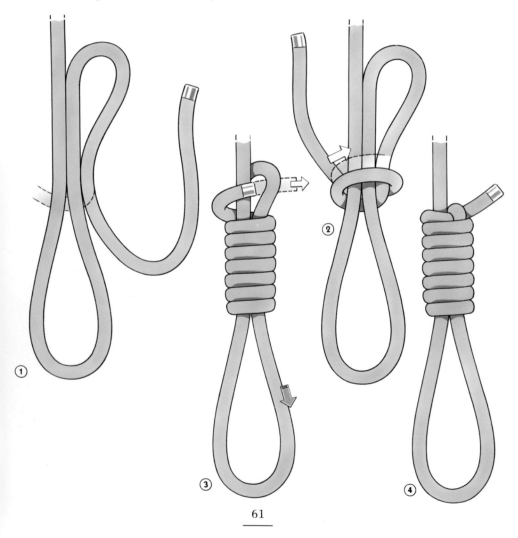

NOOSE

This simple knot can be used as the first knot in tying up a parcel. On a larger scale, it is sometimes used to put tackle cables under stress. It is made of string or small stuff.

The noose can also be used as a hitch, when it has two main functions. When a noose is tied around something large – a tree trunk, for example – only a fairly short length of line is required. If a constrictor knot or a clove or cow hitch were used, on the other hand, far more rope would be

needed. When nooses are used as hitches they are very secure.

A noose can also be used when it is difficult to get close to the object around which the knot is to be tied. It may, for instance, be possible to pass the end of a line around the base of an inaccessible object, tie a noose and tighten it.

A stopper knot should be added to prevent the noose slipping.

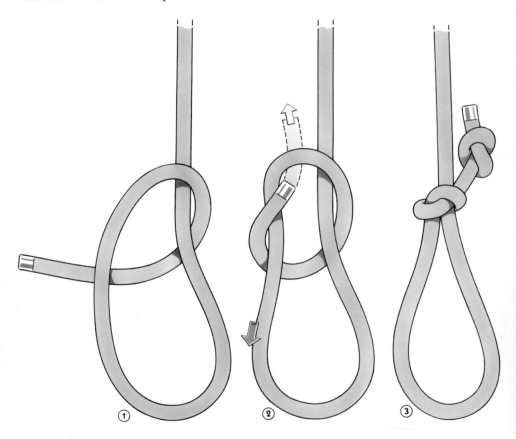

SHORTENINGS

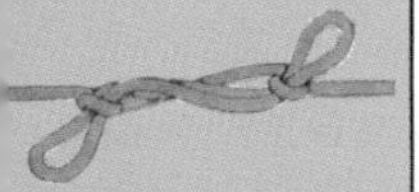

SHEEPSHANK

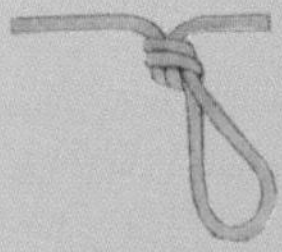

LOOP KNOT

As their name implies, these invaluable knots are used to shorten long lines. Short ropes may be needed temporarily to tow a car or haul a load, for example, and a shortened rope is always more secure than two cut lengths joined together with another knot. In any case, a longer rope may be needed at some later date, and a rope shortened by means of a knot can always be lengthened at some later date. Shortenings can also be used to take up weakened or damaged lengths of line so that they are not subjected to any strain. These knots are well worth mastering.

SHEEPSHANK

The sheepshank is a seafarer's knot: it does not chafe, it unties easily, and it has a good jamming action. It is an easily tied knot, which holds under tension – in fact, as soon as the tension is released, the knots fall apart. The number of half hitches can vary from three to five, and that number determines both the firmness of the grip of the knot and the length by which the line is shortened.

In addition to shortening lines without the need to cut them, the sheepshank is used at sea for towing boats and on the running rigging. It can also be used to keep slack lines out of the way, which could have numerous applications, including keeping bell ropes tidy. When the knot is used to shorten a damaged line, it is important that the damaged section of rope passes through both of the half hitches.

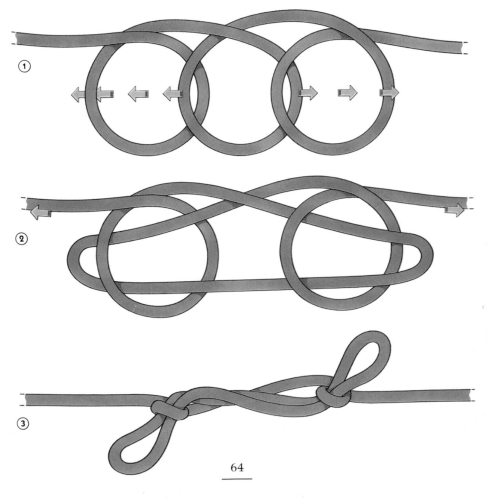

LOOP KNOT

One of the best ways of shortening a damaged rope is to tie a loop knot. This simple fastening takes up the weakened part of the line in the centre of the knot so that it is not put under strain. The knot is often used for towing cars and trucks.

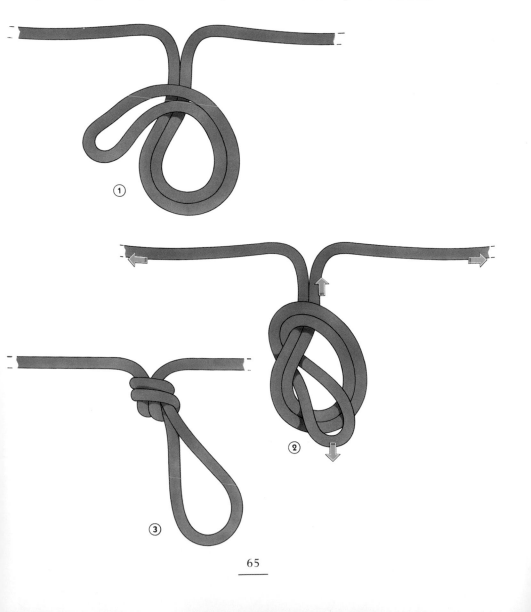

The knots used in fishing are different from those used by mariners, climbers and campers because they are tied in fine monofilament, and the very nature of monofilament means that once fastened, these knots cannot usually be untied. Each knot that a fisherman uses performs a different function, and it is possible that as many as eight knots at a time may be required. A knot may be used to join two lengths of fishing line, it may join a line to a leader, or it may attach a lure, hook sinker or swivel to a line, for example, and a knot that is perfect for one task will not necessarily serve another purpose.

When you work with monofilament you will find that moistening the line by dipping it in water or lubricating it with saliva will help you to draw it up smoothly and bed it down tightly. You will also find that a pair of pliers is essential when you are using one of the heavier monofilament lines. It is almost impossible to draw a line really tight with your bare hands. Resist the temptation to add a lubricant such as silicone to help draw the knot tight: the lubricant will remain in the knot and will add to the chances of the knot slipping while the line is in use.

The finer the gauge of line you use to tie a knot, the easier it is to draw it up tight and seat it securely. The diameter of the line may also influence the kind of knot you tie, for some knots that work well with fine monofilament cannot be drawn up tight when they are tied in heavier gauge line. Remember that when you tie two lengths of monofilament together, the knot will be more secure if the lines are made by the same manufacturer. This is the case even if you are tying together lines of different diameters. Different manufacturers produce lines that differ in the degree of stiffness, and this can affect the success of the knot.

Once the knot is firmly seated, it should be trimmed. do not try to burn the tag end as you will only weaken the knot. Use a pair of nail clippers, scissors or cutting pliers or a pair of purpose-made cutters to trim the end at an angle of 45 degrees so close to the knot that the end does not protrude. It is important the tag end does not extend; if it does, it might catch on the hook or get caught up in weeds.

You will find that some knots can withstand a considerable strain that is consistently applied while they fail when they are subjected to a sudden jerk. You can test the characteristics of different knots for yourself by asking a friend to hold the ends of some lengths of line while you pull on the other ends. Wear gloves to protect your hands when you do this.

FISHING KNOTS

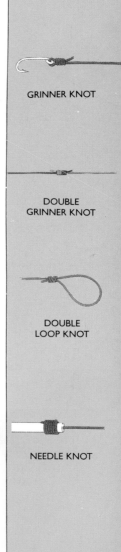

BLOOD KNOT

**BLOOD LOOP
DROPPER KNOT**

**HALF TUCKED
BLOOD KNOT**

TURLE KNOT

WATER KNOT

GRINNER KNOT

**DOUBLE
GRINNER KNOT**

**DOUBLE
LOOP KNOT**

NEEDLE KNOT

Because the conditions on a river bank may not be ideal, it is important that fishermen thoroughly master the art of tying a variety of knots before they set out. Knots must be tied securely and correctly if they are to be of any use, and wet and windy weather or poor light are not the ideal conditions in which to attempt to tie a knot for the first time. Practise tying the knots that are described on the pages that follow until you are confident that you can tie them accurately and quickly – then you are ready to tie them on the river bank.

BLOOD KNOT

Also known as: BARREL KNOT

The name barrel knot derives from the appearance of the numerous wrapping turns that are required to complete this knot, which has a relatively high breaking strain. It is widely used to tie nylon line in a host of situations, although it is most successful when the line is of more or less equal thickness.

Because anglers tie their knots in such fine line, once they are drawn up tightly it is almost impossible to untie them – the line usually has to be cut. During the 19th century, anglers and tackle makers used to be able to keep secret the intricacies of the various knots they tied because it was so difficult to unravel them.

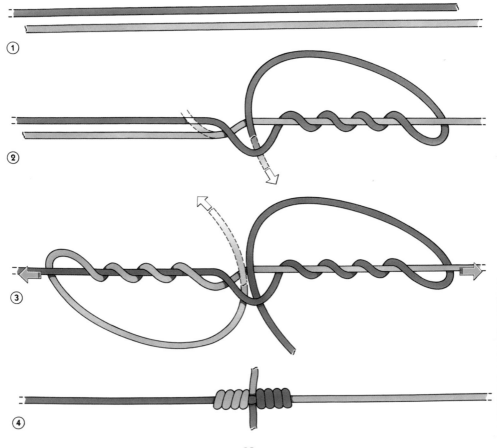

BLOOD LOOP DROPPER KNOT

Also known as: DROPPER LOOP

When fishermen want more than one fly on a line at the same time, they use a paternoster, a weighted line with a series of hooks at intervals along it. Additional flies are known as droppers, and this is the loop that is used to attach them to a paternoster because the loop is formed at a right angle to the line.

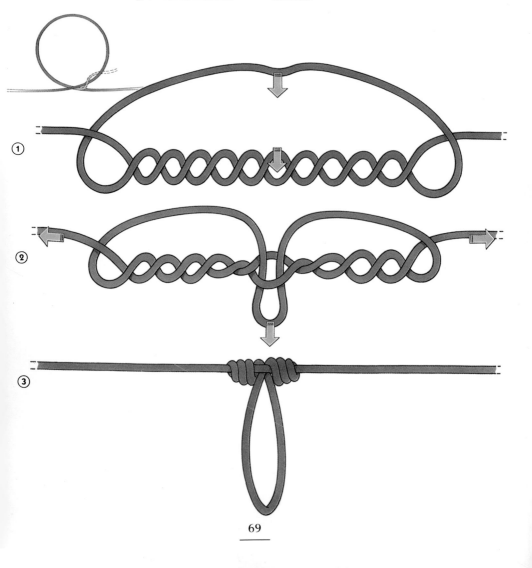

HALF-TUCKED BLOOD KNOT

Also known as: CLINCH KNOT

Anglers use this knot when they need to tie a swivel or eyed hook to their lines. It is an easy knot to master and can be tied quickly.

However, it is only really successful when it is used with fine monofilament. This is not a suitable knot for heavy lines.

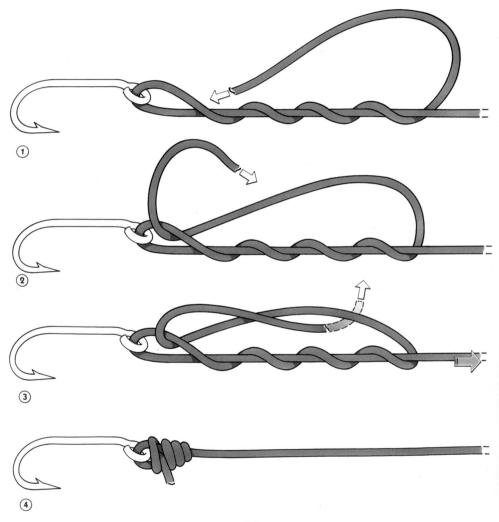

TURLE KNOT

This knot is used by fishermen to tie flies with turned-up or turned-down eyes to the tippet. It is not suitable for use with ring-eye hooks. The knot was named after Major Turle of Devon in 1884. The line is passed through the eye of the hook, the knot is tied and then the hook is drawn through the loop of the knot.

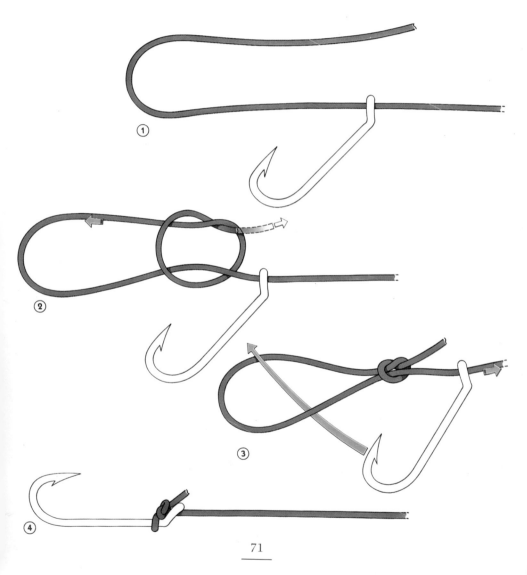

WATER KNOT

Also known as: COVE KNOT

It seems likely that this strong knot was known to Izaak Walton (1593–1683), and the earliest printed reference to it is believed to have been in 1496. It is especially useful because it can be used to join lines of different sizes, and the breaking strength can be even further enhanced by tucking the ends three more times to create a quadruple overhand knot with both lines and then drawing them carefully together as you would a multiple overhand knot (see page 17).

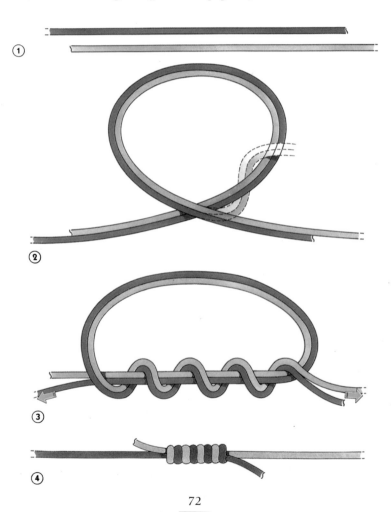

GRINNER KNOT

Also known as: DUNCAN LOOP KNOT, UNI-KNOT

This is an excellent and justifiably popular knot for joining either a fly or an eyed hook to a leader (that is, a length of nylon that forms the junction between the fly-line and the fly) or to a tippet (the thin, terminal section of a leader).

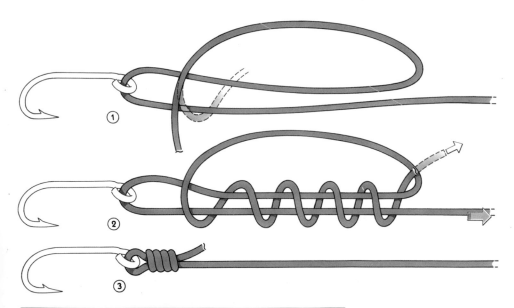

The Grinner knot and the Half-tucked blood knot are the two best methods of tying fly to line. They are difficult to master and fly fishermen will benefit from practising at home.

DOUBLE GRINNER KNOT

Also known as: PARAGUM KNOT

This knot is actually two grinner or uni-knots tied back to back. It is used by fishermen who are trying to catch large fish with small flies on very fine tippets as it is an effective way of joining together two sections of a tippet or a leader.

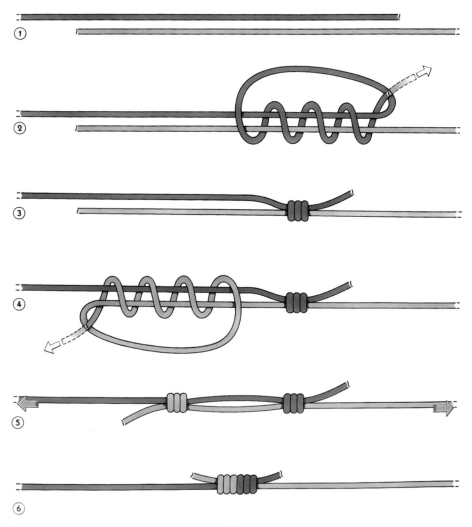

DOUBLE LOOP KNOT

Also known as: SURGEON'S LOOP

This knot is tied in the same way as the surgeon's knot (see page 52) except that it is made with a single length of line. This non-slip loop can be tied very quickly.

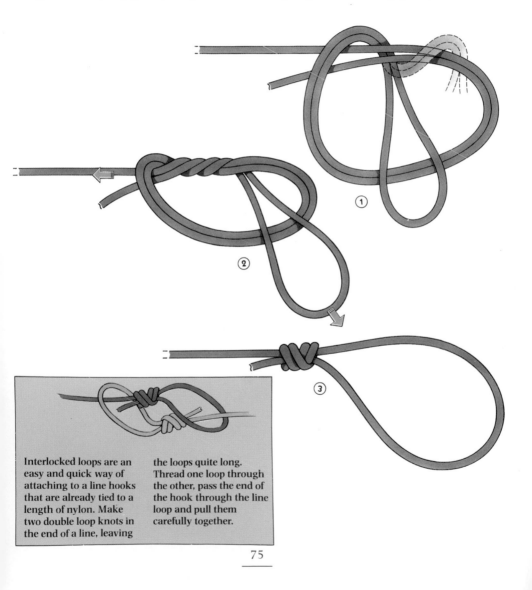

① ② ③

Interlocked loops are an easy and quick way of attaching to a line hooks that are already tied to a length of nylon. Make two double loop knots in the end of a line, leaving the loops quite long. Thread one loop through the other, pass the end of the hook through the line loop and pull them carefully together.

NEEDLE KNOT

Also known as: NEEDLE NAIL KNOT

The needle knot is used to effect a smooth join between the fly line and the butt end (that is, the thick part) of the leader. Not only is this an extremely strong way of fastening monofilament to a fly line, it is also unlikely to catch or snag on debris as the line is fished.

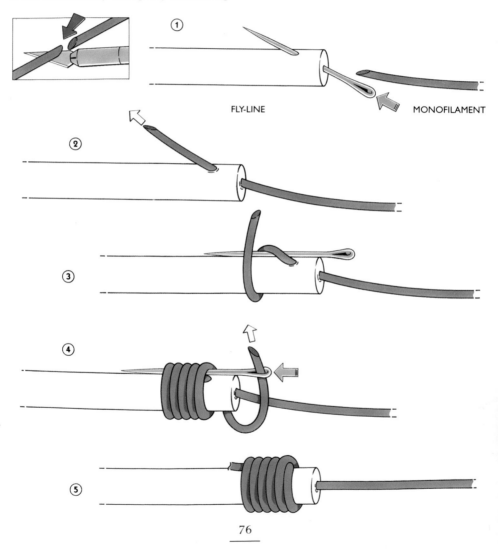

FLY-LINE

MONOFILAMENT

GLOSSARY

Backing line monofilament or a braided polyester line with a breaking strain of 7–9kg (15–19lb) used under the fly-line to bulk out a fly-reel spool. It prevents the fine fly-line from twisting and forming into tight coils. When a large fish that makes a long run is caught, the backing line can also be allowed to run out after the fly-line.

Bend the action of tying two ropes together by their ends; thus the name of various knots used to tie one rope to another or to an object.

Bight the slack section of a rope, extending from the working end to the stand end, especially when it is formed into a loop when a rope is bent back on itself. A knot tied "in the bight" or "on the bight" does not require the ends for the tying process.

Breaking strain or strength (BS) the rope manufacturer's estimate of the load that will cause a rope to part; the calculation takes no account of wear and tear, shock loading or knots, and it cannot be regarded as a safe working load. The manufacturer's calculation is based on the strength of a line when it is dry. Lines are weaker when they are knotted or wet.

Butt the thick part of a leader, the other section having been joined to the fly-line. It is usually monofilament with a breaking strain of 9–10kg (19–22lb), although braided monofilament is sometimes used.

Cable a large rope or anchor warp or chain.

Cable-laid rope formed of three right-handed hawsers laid up left-handed to form a larger, nine-stranded rope or cable.

Capsize the distortion in the shape of a knot that loosens or slips when it is under stress; some knots are deliberately capsized as a way of tying or untying them.

Clear the action of loosening tangles in ropes.

Cleat a small piece of wood or metal with projecting ends on which a rope may be fastened.

Cord several tightly twisted yarns to make a line with a diameter of less than 10mm (⅜in).

Cordage a collective name for ropes and cords, used especially to describe the ropes in a ship's rigging.

Core or heart the inner part or heart of a rope or sennet of more than three stands and in most braided lines; it is formed from a loosely twisted strand or from a bundle of parallel yarns and runs the length of larger ropes. It may be a cheap, weak filler or serve specifically as a strengthener or stiffener.

Dog the winding back of the tail end of a rope around itself or around another rope (often larger) with the lay to secure it temporarily against a lengthwise pull.

Dogged a draw loop that is prevented from undoing accidentally by whipping it or sticking something through it.

Double line similar to a loop, but both strands of line are used together rather than working with the loop that is formed.

Dropper a short length of monofilament bearing a wet fly and joined to the leader between the end fly and the fly-line. Some leaders are commercially made with droppers attached; alternatively, droppers may be attached to a plain leader by means of a blood knot (see page 68). See also team of flies, below.

Eight-plait strong but flexible rope formed from four pairs of strands, two of which spiral clockwise and two of which spiral anticlockwise; such rope does not kink.

End usually the end of a length of rope that is being knotted, but see standing end *and* working end.

Eye a loop formed at the end of a length of rope by seizing or splicing.

Fid a tapering wooden pin used to work or loosen strands of rope.

Foul a rope that cannot slide because it is tangled or caught.

Fray the unravelling, especially of the end, of a length of rope.

Grommet or **grummet** a ring, usually of twisted rope or metal, used to fasten the edge of a sail to its stay, to hold an oar in place, etc.

Hangar *see* pendant.

Hawser a rope or cable large enough for towing or mooring; it usually has a circumference of 13–60cm (5–24in).

Heart *see* core.

Hitch a knot that secures a rope to a post, ring, spar, etc. or to another rope.

Karabiner a metal coupling link with a safety closure used by mountaineers.

Kernmantel modern synthetic rope made of a smooth outer sheath of tightly braided fibres fitted over a core of filaments.

Lanyard a short rope or cord, usually three stranded and often braided or ornamented, used to secure objects or rigging or as a handle for tools and gear.

Lay the direction, either left- or right-handed, of the twist of the strands forming a rope.

Lead the direction taken by the working end through a knot.

Leader the length of nylon that forms the junction between the fly-line and the fly. It may be tapered mechanically and thus be knotless or it may be reduced in diameter by using sections of lines with different diameters. Because it is less bulky than the fly-line itself, more delicate presentation of the fly is possible. In addition, when a floating line is used, lengthening the leader makes it possible to fish in deeper water.

Line the generic name for cordage with no specific purpose, although it can be used to refer to rope with a definite use – e.g., fishing line, clothes line.

Loop a part of a rope bent so that its parts come together or cross.

Marline a thin line of two, often loosely twisted, strands, used for twisting round the ends of ropes or cables to prevent fraying.

Marling the act of lashing or binding with marline, taking a hitch at each turn.

Marlinspike or **marline spike** or **marling spike** a pointed iron instrument for separating the strands of a rope in splicing or marling.

Nip the binding pressure within a knot that prevents it from slipping.

Pendant or **hanger** a short length of rope with an eye spliced in one end and a hook in the other.

Plain-laid rope three-stranded rope, twisted – i.e., laid – to the right.

Point a conical or decorative end of a rope used to help reeve it through holes and eyes.

Reeve the act of slipping the end of a rope through a block, ring or cleat.

Rope a thick, strong cord measuring more than 2.5cm (1in) in circumference made from intertwisted strands of fibre, thin wire, leather strips, etc.

Safe working load (SWL) the estimated load that can be placed on a rope without it breaking, given its age, condition, the knots used and any shock loading. NB: safe working load may be as little as one-sixth of the manufacturer's quoted breaking strength.

Seized fastened or attached by binding with turns of yarn.

Sennit or **sinnet** braided cordage made in flat or round or square form from between three and nine cords.

Slack the part of rope that is not under tension.

S-laid rope left-handed rope.

Small stuff twine, string or cord, or rope that has a circumference of less than 2.5cm (1in) or a diameter of less than 10mm (½in).

Soft laid loosely twisted rope.

Splice the act of joining ends of rope by interweaving strands.

Standing end the short area at the end of the standing part.

Standing part the part of a rope that is fixed or under tension as opposed to the end that is free (the working end) with which the knot is tied. In fishing, the standing part is wound around the reel.

Stopper a short length of rope or chain used to limit the running of a line or to hold lines while they are cleated.

Strand yarns twisted together in the opposite direction to the yarn itself; rope made with strands (not braided) is known as laid line.

Tag end the part of a fishing line in which the knot is tied; see working end.

Team of flies two, three or four wet flies attached to the same leader by means of short lengths of monofilament (or droppers, see above). When three flies are used, the top one (which bounces off the surface of the water) is known as the bob fly or top dropper, the middle one is known as the middle dropper and the bottom one is known as the point or tail fly.

Tippet or **point** the thin, terminal section of the leader to which the fly is tied. It is usually 30–45cm (12–18in) long.

Turn one round of a rope – i.e., the basic element of the knot; a turn is usually achieved by passing the working end around the standing part or a standing loop. To take a turn is to make a single round with the rope around a cleat or bollard.

Warp the act of moving a vessel from one place in a harbour to another by means of ropes or hawsers; a warp is, thus, a rope or hawser used for that purpose.

Whipping the act of tightly wrapping small stuff around the end of a length of rope to prevent it unlaying and fraying.

Working end the part of a rope used in tying a knot; the opposite of standing end.

Yarn the basic element of a rope or cord.

Z-laid right-handed rope.

WITHDRAWN

INDEX

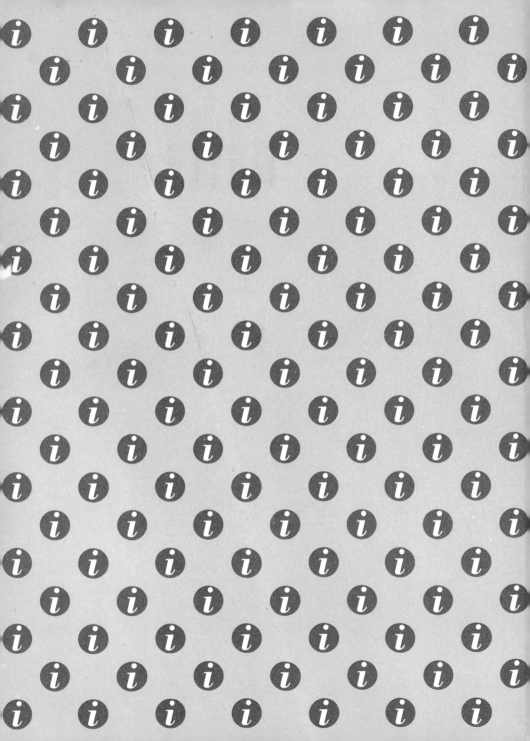